NUMBER FIVE
UNIVERSITY OF WASHINGTON CHAPBOOKS
Edited by Glenn Hughes

SINCLAIR LEWIS
Our Own Diogenes

Sinclair Lewis

Our Own Diogenes

By

VERNON LOUIS PARRINGTON

FOLCROFT LIBRARY EDITIONS

1973

SINCLAIR LEWIS
Our Own Diogenes

SINCLAIR LEWIS
Our Own Diogenes

S the row of his pudgy, orange-backed volumes lengthens on the shelf, it becomes evident that Sinclair Lewis is the bad boy of American letters whose thoughts are on bent-pins while the deacon is labouring in prayer. His irrepressible satire belongs to a new and irritatingly effective school. He has studied the technique of the realists, and under the beguiling pretense of telling the truth objectively and dispassionately, he insists on revealing to us unaccommodated man as a poor, bare, forked animal, who like Jurgen persists in thinking himself a monstrous clever fellow. He is maliciously severe on all respectable dignities. In his hands the noble *homo sapiens* of common repute is translated into an ignoble *homo libidinus et ventosissimus*—an unattractive animal that runs in herds, serves its belly, and has a taking way with the dams. The free-born American citizen, master of the earth and its destiny, is little flattered by the portrait he draws, and Mr. Lewis finds

7

himself, in consequence, *persona non grata* in any
convention of Elks or Rotarians.

The method he has chosen to adopt is a clever
advance over the technique of the eighteenth century, when pricking balloons was the business of
every wit. Those older satirists—nagging souls
like Pope and bold bad fellows like Churchill—
were mainly concerned to annoy their victims with
pin-pricks. They were too completely the gentleman to grow chummy with base fellows whom
they frankly despised; and in consequence they
never discovered half the possibilities of the gentle
art of satire. Sinclair Lewis is wiser than they
were. He has learned that before one can effect-
ively impale one's victim, one must know all his
weaknesses and take him off his guard. So he
ingratiatingly makes up to George F. Babbitt of
Zenith, drinks chummily with him, swaps greasy
jokes, learns all the hidden vanities and secret
obscenities that slip out in the confidences of the
cups, beguiles him into painting his own portrait
in the manly midnight hours; and when the last
garment that covers his nakedness is stripped off,
the flashlight explodes and the camera has caught
the victim in every feature of his mean and
vacuous reality.

No doubt it is an ungentlemanly thing to do—a calculating betrayal of trusting human nature done in the sacred name of art; and it is certain that the unhappy victim will hate the artist when he sees the developed print next morning. Yet the picture is extraordinarily life-like. All the unlovely details of fat stomach and flabby muscles are sharply revealed. It is too late to put on one's clothes, and *homo sapiens* in the person of George F. Babbitt is revealed as a shambling, two-legged animal, for the world to laugh at. The method is immensely clever; it is the last word in the technique of despoiling one's victim of adventitious dignity, without which life becomes a mean, bleak affair; but it is scarcely charitable. To think well of oneself and to wish to impose that good opinion upon others, are common human weaknesses that every tailor blesses. Without clothes man is only a caricature of the godlike, and the artist who betrays our nakedness to our enemies is very far from a gentleman. The confidences of the cups must be held sacred, for if we cannot drink without fear of our babbling being reported, what becomes of goodfellowship?

But the charge of betraying goodfellowship leaves Sinclair Lewis unconcerned. His satire

knows no compunctions. An irreverent soul, he
not only dares the wrath of George F. Babbitt,
but of the innumerable clubs to which Babbitt belongs. A buoyant scoffer, he does not permit even
the organized wrath of the Chamber of Commerce
to disturb his equanimity. He provokes respectable people on principle, and he has laid a devilish
plan to work systematically through our sacred
American decalogue, smashing one commandment
after another. Already behind him is strewn a
sorry wreckage of established creeds and authoritative slogans—a wreckage that delights the
wicked and gives aid and comfort to all evil-
wishers in our comfortable and excellent society.
Not even a banker is sacred to him. Rotarians and
Kiwanians, Billy Sundays and Billy Bryans,
voluble congressmen and silent presidents, even
our venerable Constitution itself, he scoffs at and
makes merry over. And to add insult to injury,
he prospers in his sins. His calculating wickedness
returns him a fattening bank account. His impu-
dent satires sell like bargain-counter silk stockings.
We pay handsomely to see ourselves most un-
handsomely depicted. If we would only take a
lesson from the strategy of the heathen Chinese,
we might boycott Mr. Lewis's wares and reduce

him to the beggary that is more becoming to
wickedness than a wanton prosperity. But a
Christian people will not go to school to the
heathen, and so Mr. Lewis prospers in his wickedness and waxes vulgarly rich.

Now what is the tremendous discovery that
Sinclair Lewis makes so much of, and that we pay
so great a price to learn?   It is no other than this:
that the goodly United States of America are
peopled by a mighty herd, which like those earlier
herds that rumbled about the plains, drives fool-
ishly in whatever direction their noses point—a
herd endowed with tremendous blind power, with
big bull leaders, but with minds rarely above their
bellies and their dams.   In the mass and at their
own romantic rating they are distinctly imposing
—big-necked, red-blooded, lusty, with glossy
coats got from rich feeding grounds, and with a
herd power that sweeps majestically onward in a
cloud of dust of its own raising, veritable lords and
masters of a continent.   But considered more
critically and resolved into individual members,
they appear to the realist somewhat stupid, feeble
in brain and will, stuffed with conceit of their own

excellence, esteeming themselves the great end for
which creation has been in travail, the finest handiwork of the Most High who spread the plains for
their feeding. grounds: with a vast respect for
totems and fetishes; purveyors and victims of the
mysterious thing called Bunk, who valiantly horn
to death any audacious heretic who may suggest
that rumbling about the plains, filling their bellies,
bellowing sacred slogans, and cornering the lushest
grass, are scarcely adequate objectives for such im-
mense power: a vast middleman herd, that domi-
nates the continent, but cannot reduce it to order or
decency.

Consider, suggests Mr. Lewis, what this rumbling herd signifies in the light of rational and
humane ideals. What sort of custodians of civilization are these lumbering mobsters with their
back-slappings and bellowings? What becomes of
the good life in a society that flowers in Rotarian
conventions? The banker has reduced America to
the level of a banker's Utopia, and now bids us
admire his handiwork. Other societies, aristocratic
and feudal, honoured the priest and knight and
artist above the usurer and tradesman; other generations professed to serve truth and beauty and

godliness in their daily lives; but the great American herd cares nothing for such things. In the name of democracy priest and knight and artist are turned lackeys to merchants and realtors, to men who would not recognize faith or chivalry or imagination if they met them on the golf course, and who understand democracy as little as they understand Christianity. In this land of material abundance the good life is reduced to being measured in commissions and percentages; civilization comes to flower in the broker; the mahogany desk is the altar at which we sacrifice in a land of triumphant materialism. "God help the country," said Fenimore Cooper, years ago when the herd was small, "that has only commercial towns for its capitals." "Such a country is past helping," retorts Sinclair Lewis. "God cannot help it, or the Devil. In the name of George F. Babbitt and Dr. Almus Pickerbaugh and the Reverend Elmer Gantry, what can be expected of such a country? A people that worships the great god Bunk shall have its reward!"

To prove his amiable thesis Mr. Lewis has been at enormous pains to gather his materials at their sources. He has taken upon himself to become a

specialist in depicting the *genus americanus*. He
has loafed along Main Street, played poker in back
rooms with wicked young men, drunk in respectable clubs, and exchanged hearty back-slappings
with the sons of Rotary. He has devoted days to
the smoking compartments of Pullmans, garnering
the ripest wisdom and choicest stories of travelling
salesmen. He has listened to philosophic brokers
discourse on ethics, studied political and constitu-
tional theory with realtors, learned all about
Bolshevism from presidents of Chambers of
Commerce, been instructed in the elements of
economics by Republican congressmen, discovered
the fallacies in Darwinian evolution from clerical
fundamentalists and the superiority of Fascism
over democracy from the greatest captains of in-
dustry. No field of American experience has
escaped his minute investigation, no authority has
eluded his catechising. In the course of his studies
he has come to master the lusty American language
in its subtlest shades and manliest *nuances*, from
the comic supplement to Dunn and Bradstreet, and
he talks easily with Main Street in its own ver-
nacular. His rich and copious vocabulary fills a
commonplace scholar with envy, and his ebullient
slang, his easy slovenliness of enunciation, inflict

on the simple-minded user of the King's English
a hopeless inferiority complex.

Thus amply equipped with all the resources of
scholarship, he has written four learned treatises
in exemplification of the thesis that the *genus
americanus* is cousin german to the scoffing Mr.
Mencken's lately discovered *boobus americanus*.
The introductory study, *Main Street*, provided a
comprehensive background and setting for the
full-length portraits he was to draw later. Gopher
Prairie, situated in the heart of agricultural
America—in Meredith Nicholson's Valley of
Democracy where the old-fashioned, kindly,
neighborly, wholesome, democratic virtues are
presumed to thrive in a congenial habitat—becomes
in his unsympathetic analysis a place that William
Allen White would not recognize as his home
town. Here, he tells us, is respectability made
sluggish and sterile. Here is "slavery self-sought
and self-defended." Here is "dullness made
God." Here, diluted and spread over a vast ter-
ritory, the spirit of Babbitt has erupted in cheap
and pretentious county-seats, parasites on the
producing hinterland over whose politics and
credit and morals Main Street tradesmen have set
up a strict custodianship—futile and complacent

and drab, mere echoes of the greater cities that lie
on the horizon and to which the sons of Main
Street turn for light and guidance.

It is these greater cities that constitute the true
capitals of our red-blooded Americans who pro-
claim themselves "the greatest race in the world"
—fruitful centres from which radiates the philosophy of pep, punch and progress for the upbuilding and enlightenment of the world. Of
these centres the hustling and mighty Zenith is the
wonder and admiration of all right-minded citizens; it is the brightest and bloomiest sunflower of
the great American garden. And in Zenith dwells
George F. Babbitt, realtor, Sinclair Lewis's full-
length portrait of a hero sprung from the loins of
America, the completest embodiment of the triumphant American genius that is conquering the
earth. Babbitt as an up-standing he-member of
the great herd, is a marvel, the apotheosis of the
regnant middle-class, the finished product of our
snappy civilization. Other lands, no doubt, have
produced men accounted great. Plato and Saul of
Tarsus, Saint Francis and Leonardo, Pascal and
Galileo and Hegel, were no doubt esteemed in
their own times and by their own cities; but
Zenith does not go in for out-of-date merchandise;

it is up-to-the-minute and it specializes in George
F. Babbitts. And so when the Reverend Elmer
Gantry rises to influence in Gopher Prairie, he is
called to Zenith as its spiritual counsellor, and becomes the custodian of the Zenith moralities, the
apostle of Zenith Bunk, the devotee of the Zenith
Mumbo Jumbo. And through Zenith passes also
Martin Arrowsmith the rebel, the perverse out-
landish scientist who refuses to worship Mumbo
Jumbo, on his solitary way to discover reality in a
world of Zenith chicanery. Babbitt, Gantry, Arrowsmith—these are the figures that Sinclair Lewis
comes upon in his exploration of the land of the
free and the home of the brave. A somewhat
curious showing at the best.

So slashing an attack upon our common creed
and practice has naturally aroused vigorous pro-
test. Human nature does not like to have its idols
assailed; even the devotees of Mumbo Jumbo will
defend their god against the heretics; and Sinclair
Lewis has become the target for many a shaft.
The critics have pressed home their counter attack
with ardour. They insist that he is suffering from
an aggravated case of astigmatism, and that in
consequence he does not see eye to eye with those

of normal vision. The world is out of focus to him—askew in all its structural lines; and this distorted vision prompts those jaundiced opinions and malicious judgments in regard to the ideals cherished by our best citizens. He has deliberately cultivated a spleen that makes him dislike his neighbors because they are comfortable and contented. Diogenes railing at mankind gained a vast reputation, but it is a nice question if Diogenes was a useful citizen. What did he do to further the well-being of his community? How much time and money did he give to charity and the upbuilding of his city? For all his talking Mr. Lewis does not seem to know what the good life is. He rails at Babbitt for not being Plato, but does he understand the ABC of service? To take a homely figure: the family cow, standing knee-deep in June and chewing the cud of contentment, would excite his Diogenic scorn. As a fault-finder and knocker, Brindle is not the equal of Diogenes; but to criticize her mentality and manners, forgetful of the fact that from the contented chewing of a plentiful cud will come a plentiful supply of milk and cream and butter to sweeten the bread of life, is a somewhat sorry business. In her modest, democratic sphere she is devoted to service, and if

there is a nobler function, Rotary humbly confesses
it has not discovered it.   One must not, of course,
press too far the analogy between Brindle and
Babbitt; the figure is useful only to suggest that
even in the lowliest spheres Mr. Lewis completely
fails to understand the fine ethical values that
underlie and animate the common American life
at which he rails.   How, then, shall he understand
them in the higher?   Comfort and service are excellent things in themselves, and if they can be
merged in everyday experience, surely the good
life is in the way of achievement.

The point is of vast importance, for it is here
that Diogenes Lewis, his critics assert, has totally
misread the meaning and faith of America.   Here
in this prosperous land the union between comfort
and service—or to put it in more dignified phrase,
the synthesis of Hellenism and Hebraism—has
been achieved in practice.   A rich and abundant
life, motivated by a fine sense of ethical responsi-
bility and disciplined by a democratic public school,
is, in sober fact, the distinguishing characteristic of
America that sets our country apart from all other
lands in western civilization.   Call it a Babbitt
warren if you will, nevertheless where else has the
industrial revolution been brought so completely

and happily under dominion to the democratic
ideal, or been so ennobled by ethical values? Here
it has scattered its wealth amongst the plain people
with a bountiful hand, until the poorest family
enjoys its nickel-plated plumbing, its flivver, its
telephone, its radio, its movies, its funnies, and all
the thousand aids to comfort and intelligence
which a few generations ago were denied kings—
the result of all which is a standard of living that
our forefathers would have envied. Our Hellenism is, happily, not Greek. That, as every school
boy in America knows, was established in slavery;
whereas our modern Hellenism is established in
democracy and ennobled by a sensitive social
conscience. Here the master serves. The richest
and greatest amongst us—our Judge Garys and
Andrew Mellons—are servants of the nameless
public, and dedicate their creative genius to the
common democratic prosperity. Our Hellenism,
in short, is engrafted on a sturdy Hebraic root and
flowers in righteousness—in charity, in education,
in free clinics and hospitals, in scientific founda-
tions, in great public libraries, in all the vast gifts
that wealth freely offers to the cause of social
amelioration. The Puritan strain is fortunately
still the American strain, and we owe much to

those excellent origins that Mr. Lewis scoffs at
without understanding. Comfort and service—
Hellenism and Hebraism: if this is not the good
life, where shall one find it?   In Bolshevic Russia?
After all Diogenes Lewis is no more important—
or useful—than the gad-fly that Brindle brushes
from her glossy sides as she chews her cud. What
gad-fly ever produced butter?

If Sinclair Lewis is unimpressed by such argu-
ments it is because he is quite disillusioned with the
current ideal of material progress. His dreams
do not find their satisfaction in good roads and
cheap gasoline. He would seem to be an incor-
rigible idealist who has been bred up on the
vigorous Utopianisms of the late nineteenth century. In the golden days before the deluge he
had gone blithely to school to all the current
idealisms that flourished in the land—to Jeffer-
sonian democracy and to Marxian socialism; and
in the well-stocked pharmacopeias of hopeful
young liberals he professed to discover specifics
for all our social ills. But the war destroyed his
faith in nostrums and removed his Utopia to a
dim and foggy future. He has not yet travelled
so far in disillusion as Mr. Cabell, who has seen

fit to dwarf man to the compass of a flea on the
epidermis of earth; nor has he achieved the irony
—or the technique—of Clarence Darrow, who
suggests casually: "Of course I know that Confucius was as great a philosopher as Billy Sunday,
and that as a thinker Buddha was the equal of
Billy Bryan. But still all orthodox people know
that Confucius and Buddha were spurious and the
Billy brothers genuine." He has not even achieved
the smug satisfaction of the psychologists who impose their preposterous intelligence tests on simple
folk and triumphantly discover morons in respectable neighbours. Some lingering faith in our poor
human nature he still clings to. In the great
American mass that human nature is certainly
foolish and unlovely enough. It is too often
blown up with flatulence, corroded with lust, on
familiar terms with chicanery and lying; it openly
delights in hocus pocus and discovers its miracle
workers in its Comstocks and Aimee Semple Mc-
Phersons. But for all its pitiful flabbiness human
nature is not wholly bad, nor is man so helpless a
creature of circumstance as the cynics would have
us believe. There are other and greater gods than
Mumbo Jumbo worshipped in America, worthier
things than hocus pocus; and in rare moments even

Babbitt dimly perceives that the feet of his idol are clay. There are Martin Arrowsmiths as well as Elmer Gantrys, and human nature, if it will, can pull itself out of the trap. Bad social machinery makes bad men. Put the banker in the scullery instead of the drawing-room; exalt the test-tube and deflate the cash-register; rid society of the dictatorship of the middle class; and the artist and the scientist will erect in America a civilization that may become, what civilization was in earlier days, a thing to be respected. For all his modernity and the disillusion learned from Pullman-car philosophers, Sinclair Lewis is still an echo of Jean Jacques and the golden hopes of the Enlightenment—thin and far-off, no doubt, but still an authentic echo.

Whether we like Mr. Lewis's technique or not, whether we agree with his indictment of middle-class ideals or dissent from it, his writings are suggestive documents symptomatic of a dissatisfied generation given over to disillusion. The optimistic dreams of middle-class capitalism are not so golden as they seemed to us before the war; and these pudgy, yellow-backed novels are slashing attacks on a world that in mouthing empty shibboleths is only whistling to keep up its courage. The

faith of America is dead. These brisk pages are
filled with the doings of automata—not living
men but the simulacra of men, done with astonish-
ing verisimilitude, speaking an amazingly realistic
language, professing a surprising lifelikeness; yet
nevertheless only shells from which the life has
departed, without faith or hope or creative energy,
not even aware that they are dead.

It is this consciousness of sketching in a morgue
that differentiates Mr. Lewis from the earlier
satirists of middle-class America, who in the hopeful years before the war were busily engaged in
rebuilding the American temple. The preceding
generation—earnest souls like Robert Herrick and
Jack London and Upton Sinclair—were as well
aware of the shortcomings of our industrial order
as Sinclair Lewis, and hated them as vigorously.
From the days of Emerson and George Ripley, of
Carlyle and Ruskin, capitalistic society had been
persistently subjected to sharp and devastating
analysis; its drabness and regimentation, its
sterility and emptiness and joylessness, had been
pointed out by many pens. The Victorians long
ago discovered that no generous or humane civilization was to be expected from the hands of
Plugson of Undershot—that the banker conceiving

of human felicity in terms of eight per cent. is a
mean and shabby fellow in comparison with Saint
Francis or Michelangelo. Long before Sherwood
Anderson, William Morris had observed that the
workman no longer sings in the factory as in other
days he sang over his tool, and concluded that the
creation of beauty is more important for human
happiness than figuring profits from mass pro-
duction.

But those earlier analysts were dealing with
causes of which they could only forecast the ultimate consequences, whereas Sinclair Lewis is
dealing with effects. Plugson of Undershot is
now the universal dictator. Before the war there
was still life and hope in western civilization; it
was not yet reduced to being a common Babbitt
warren, with its Billy Sundays and Almus Picker-
baughs, its artists and editors and scientists, on the
Plugson payroll. What emerges from the drab
pages of Sinclair Lewis that is suggestive, is the
authoritative pronouncement that the effects forecast by the earlier critics have become in our day
the regnant order of things. Babbitt is the son of
Plugson of Undershot, and Babbitt is a walking
corpse who refuses to be put decently away to make
room for living men. An empty soul, he is the

symbol of our common emptiness. Historically
he marks the final passing in America of the civilization that came from the fruitful loins of the
eighteenth century. For a hundred and fifty years
western civilization had sustained its hopes on the
rich nourishment provided by the great age of the
Enlightenment. Faith in the excellence of man,
in the law of progress, in the ultimate reign of
justice, in the conquest of nature, in the finality
and sufficiency of democracy, faith in short in the
excellence of life, was the great driving force in
those earlier, simpler days. It was a noble dream
—that dream of the Enlightenment—but it was
slowly dissipated by an encompassing materialism
that came likewise out of the eighteenth century.
Faith in machinery came to supersede faith in man;
the Industrial Revolution submerged the hopes of
the French Revolution. And now we have fallen
so low that our faith in justice, progress, the poten-
tialities of human nature, the excellence of
democracy, is stricken with pernicious anemia, and
even faith in the machine is dying. Only science
remains to take the place of the old romantic creed,
and science with its psychology and physics is fast
reducing man to a complex bundle of glands, at
the mercy of a mechanistic universe. Babbitt, to

be sure, has not yet discovered the predicament he is in, but Martin Arrowsmith knows; and while Babbitt is whistling somewhat futilely, Arrowsmith is hard at work in the laboratory seeking a new philosophy to take the place of the old. The outlook is not promising, but until a new faith emerges from the test-tube Sinclair Lewis will wander in the fogs of disillusion.

But enough of such crape-hanging at a time when our best minds are engaged in the great work of stabilizing prosperity. What are test-tubes in comparison with the infallible statistics patriotically disseminated by the National City Bank? To parade such heresies in the face of the progressive American public is enough to damn any man, genius or not. We want no carpers or cynics in our congenial membership. We must all get together to put across the drive for a bigger and richer and better America; and so, reluctantly, despite the fact that in many ways he is a good fellow, we blackball Sinclair Lewis.